Why Not Turn Your Ideas Into E-Book

How To Discover The Writing Creativity In Your, Write Your Own Book And Publish It!

It's Easier Than You Think...

Most people who are new to the Internet, or even some who have been around for a while, believe that they can't create their own eBooks (or CD''s, videos, etc.) because they can't write.

There are also a lot of 'so-called' gurus or experts who want you to believe that it's more difficult than it actually is.

In this report you'll learn that you CAN create your own eBooks and other products. And that you can do it **fast**! It doesn't even matter if you have any writing experience. Your main challenge will be to prove that you're an expert on the topic you're writing about. But don't worry; creating your own product will be easy once you learn the shortcut and tips outlined below.

It's about perspective. Imagine if you'd never seen a bicycle before and then suddenly you saw someone riding one. You'd think, wow, that's incredible, there's no way I can do that. But you can. Sure it'll take some practice and some instruction. And for the first bit, if someone runs beside you – that would make it easier. That's what this eBook is, it's that first help you need to be on your way. Writing something that's marketable is possible and you can learn how. It's just like riding a bike.

The trick really is to just get started. An empty page will kill your creativity. Just start writing and let your thoughts flow. At the beginning, don't worry about spelling, grammar, sentence structure or formatting. Just get the information **out** of you. The editing comes later. If you edit while you write, you'll interrupt your flow of ideas.

You could also try recording yourself. Talk freely and imagine you're talking to a friend. Give advice about the subject your writing about. Then, when you're done, you can type it all out into your computer, or get someone to transcribe it.

You don't need to be an English major to write an eBook. In fact it's better if you're not. The best writing and the easiest to read is conversational. Write the way you talk to a friend, and don't try to impress with fancy words. Then, read it out loud. This is super important. You'll find things you won't see by reading it silently. And before you know it you'll be adding, editing, and moving content around. You can also hire a college student to edit it for you, if you're not comfortable doing it yourself. EBooks that feel like the author is talking to the reader are the most helpful and easiest to read, even if a comma is in the wrong spot. Perfect can be perfectly *boring*. So don't get hung up on grammatical details.

If it still seems like a daunting task to write the book, break the eBook up into sections or chapters, and knock them out one at a time. Think of it as writing short reports. Write a list of all the different areas you want to cover. Then write about them one at a time. Don't stress about flow. You can move the order around later. The first step is the content. You'll be amazed at how easy it is to put it all together once you've got lots to work with.

Another Alternative

If you still want an easier or different way to do it, hire *someone else* to write it for you. You can go to a site like elance.com and find a ghostwriter.

Hundreds of marketers are releasing products every day using the above strategy. They didn't write a word of it, and they not even an expert on the subject but they are still making profits from it! It's the easiest way to start into this business and begin making money quickly!

How To Create Products In A Matter Of Hours!

Creating products is easy; all you have to do is break away from the limitations of the 'standard' way of creating things.

In other words, you don't have to do all the work yourself! In fact, if you get a little creative, you won't have to do *any* of the work!

You don't even have to know a thing about the subject that you'd like to create a product on.

The tips and strategies provided below will definitely get your brain firing on overtime. ;-)

Interview An Expert

The fastest and easiest way to come up with a high-value product is to interview an expert on the subject that you want to write about. How do you get this expert to talk to you? Easy, you ask them. After all, by using their name in your eBook, they're getting free exposure and publicity. Plus people are flattered when they're asked to be interviewed; it's a compliment on their talents. Your interviewee will enjoy talking about their area of expertise, it's their passion, and they'll love sharing it with you as long as you appear enthusiastic and gracious.

You can also interview several experts and compile all the interviews into one product, in order to cover different angles and strategies on one subject. Or, you could pick a general subject, break that up into sub-sections and then interview an expert for each sub-section. For example, if you're creating a product on 'Internet Business Success,' you could interview an expert on product creation, another on copywriting, one on marketing strategies, and so on. Your interview can include a set of specific questions, or just one question that requires a detailed answer.

You could also ask the expert to offer you a step-by-step plan that readers would be able to follow to get to their goal. The easier you make it for the reader, the more likely will he be to buy your product.

There are various formats you could choose to conduct and publish the interviews. You could simply send the questions to them via email and publish the answers into a report or eBook format. You could also choose to meet the expert one-on-one and record the interview, or you could conduct the interview over the phone and record it that way.

If you choose to record the interviews, your product package could then contain the audios as well as the typed up transcripts. Or if you choose to video tape the interview you could sell copies of the recorded video. Your pricing would vary depending on which formats of your products you provide.

Record Your Own Tips and Advice

If you're an expert in a subject yourself there are quite a few ways you can market your knowledge. One option is to get someone to ask you preset questions and record/transcribe those. You could also do a free or paid tele-seminar, record that and turn that into an instant product. Offer it as downloadable audios, an actual CD, or just the typed up transcripts. A similar strategy can be used on live seminars. You can either video tape the seminar; make an audio recording of it, or both.

Consider inviting other experts to join you in the seminar, than turn that into an instant product. These days" webcasts are also popular. It's simply a seminar via the Internet. Easily recorded then transferred into another product.

Turn Existing Content Into Products

You could easily contact a whole array of experts and ask them to submit their best articles or reports on a particular subject. Then, compile them into a larger report or even an eBook. Each expert gets to include their web links at the end of their content so they get free publicity from the submission. It's a win-win situation.

You could expand the exposure of your newly created product by giving all the experts who participated, the chance to sell the product to their own customers. You can also use this strategy with interviews as well. This is called a joint venture it and will expand your customer base quickly which means increased sales for you.

The same idea can be used to borrow or reprint sections of eBooks, audios, or even existing videos. Contact the author and ask for permission to reprint the content in exchange for free publicity.

If you want to create a product for the 'copywriting' crowd, you could contact several copywriting experts and ask them to submit a sales letters that they wrote for one of their products. You could compile all the submitted letters into one mega collection of "proven sales letters." You've got an instant product! Take this idea further still and ask each expert to break the letter apart and explain the specific techniques they used to create it. That added information could easily double or triple the value of your 'proven sales letters' package. Now think of other markets that would find expert advice invaluable and you're on your way to making tons of money.

Update/Republish Existing Information

Find an eBook/manual that's at least a year old and ask the author/publisher to update the information. For example, you could approach the author of a "free classifieds" directory and offer to help update the information to include all the new resources that came about since the directory was last published.

You could also approach the author of a printed product and ask to convert his product into an audio CD...or visa versa. Or how about taking an eBook on 'general gardening tips' and modifying it for the '*vegetable* gardening' market?

Co-Create A Product

Another way to save time is to ask an expert to co-create a product with you. If it's an informational product, you could both write it together, and split the workload. The product would be finished in half the time. The same can be done by involving several experts/authors. Each one would get assigned a portion of the work, say one chapter per author, if it were an informational product.

Help Finish Incomplete Projects

Most successful product creators, especially informational product creators, have at least one unfinished product. You can offer to help them finish it. The profits and exposure can be shared between the two of you. This can be applied to eBooks, reports, manuals, manuscripts, even software/scripts or non-informational products.

Purchase 'Private Label' Rights

You could either search for owners who are already offering private label rights to their products, or approach authors and ask for it. Private label rights offer you the right to insert 'your name' as the author of the product. You don't have to write a single word except type in your name and website information. You could either pay for these rights with cash, or barter/trade using your own products and/or reprint rights.

Hands-On Video Or Camtasia Presentations

Another super easy way to create a high-value product is to create a "how-to" video or computer presentation simply by recording yourself (or an expert) <u>while</u> working on the project. For example, you could create a "how to" product that teaches others to use/learn the features of Microsoft Word by recording yourself using MS Word and explaining the features.

Create A Package Using Existing Products
Approach several product owners and ask them to donate their product to your project, in exchange for publicity and a cut of the profits. Once you have a bunch of products from different owners, package them together and sell the bundle for an attractive price. Also, allow each owner/participant to promote the site to their own customers for a cut of the profits. It doesn't cost you a thing AND you get to build your own list fast!

Public Domain Information

This is another strategy/topic that's hot right now. Look for public domain information and republish, re-author, re-title and/or repackage it. You could also go after out-of-print informational products and work out a deal with the original publishers/authors.

Case Studies

Ask several experts to offer a case study of their most recent project. For example, if you're writing about press releases, you would ask each contributor to give you a copy of their last 'successful' press release and explain the what/why/how of the reason for its success. Compile the case studies into a guide that you can sell.

Checklists and/or "Top 10" Lists

Create or ask an expert to put together a simple checklist that one could use as a guide. For example, you could put together a 'travel checklist", which travelers could use to ensure that they have everything they need before they leave. You could also use the same idea to create a "Top 10..." list for any subject. Example: "Top 10 Ways To Increase Your Website's Profits," etc.

Sell Your Ideas

Instead of creating the products yourself, you could put together a report that lists all of your creative ideas, so that others could use them to create their own products (kind of like this list. ;-) You could even create a membership site where you share one or more new ideas each month.

Hold A Contest

If you'd like to write a report/eBook on 'creative landscape designs,' you could hold a contest and ask everyone to submit their best ideas/designs and allow you reprint rights to the submissions. Then, compile all the submissions into one report/eBook. Make sure you state on the entry form that all ideas will be published.

Templates, Forms, etc.

Create templates for others to use, compile a bunch of them together to create an instant product. Example: If you're a graphic designer, you could create eBook templates, header templates, web site templates, etc. If you're a copywriter, you could offer several web copy templates that people could use to easily create their own sales letters, etc. You could do the same thing with commonly used business letters, forms, etc.

Resources List

You could very easily compile list of useful resources on certain subjects and turn that into a product. Example: a list of free advertising sites, article submission sites, free hosting or free web space sites, free clipart, free auto responders, etc.

Directories and Guides

You could also create a directory of sites, resources, software or even businesses. For example, you could create a list of the best restaurants in your area and offer some information on each, as well as dining tips, and so on.

Capitalize on Trends and Fads

Here's an easy way to create a hot-seller. When the 'Lord of the Rings' craze hit the big screen, people started selling anything and everything that even remotely tied to the movies in some way. Fans bought 'em all! The same happened with 'Sideways' and the wine craze, Aitkin''s diet craze, and every other fad or trend that hit mainstream media. What current hot trend or fad could you attach to <u>your</u> product?

Your product doesn't even have to be an actual product! You could just as easily compile a bunch of powerful testimonials about someone else's hot product, add your affiliate links to it and pass the document around. Allow others to pass it around freely as well. Pretty soon your little report of testimonials can start earning you commissions.

Yes, it can be that easy, if you decide to make it that easy. Remember; don't let how 'most people' create products limit <u>your</u> creativity and options.

Coming Up With Winning EBook Ideas

The standard way to come up with a winning eBook idea is to study your market. Find out what the problems and frustrations of your market are and pick a subject that people are desperately needing answers to.

You can also simply "ask" people what they want. If you already have a customer base, just ask them what kind of product they're most interested in and are willing to pay for. Then, create that product for them.

The best way to ensure your eBook's success is to choose topics that provide solutions to existing problems.

But there's an easier way!

I don't particularly like to work hard unless I absolutely have to. So, if there's a shortcut to be found, I'll find it - or I'll create one! Whenever I want to create a new product, I just look at <u>what's already selling **well** out there</u> and I give that product/idea a unique twist.

Just follow the experts and top sellers, watch what's hot on Clickbank.com's Marketplace (i.e. what sells the most,) check out Amazon.com and see what's moving there. Go to forums and look for common problems or complaints people are having.

Here are a few more resources you can use to do research for your product:

Copernic 2000 - This is a free software that searches multiple search engines simultaneously to find what you're looking for.

http://www.copernic.com/

DataGrabber - This tool targets hundreds of public databases to dig up information.

http://www.wildcowpublishing.com/datagrab.html

Deja.com - allows you to search lots of usenet newsgroups simultaneously.

http://deja.com

Forum One - If you need to search through forums and message boards, this is your best bet.

http://forumone.com

Encyclopedia.com - Obviously this site allows you to search through their massive database of articles, at no charge.

http://www.encyclopedia.com/

NewsDirectory.com

Look at hundreds of newspapers all over the world.

http://www.newsdirectory.com/news/press/

Establish Your Uniqueness!

Creating products is not difficult. But if you really want to make good money in this business and establish yourself as a respected expert, you have to be unique! This is so important that it's worth repeating several times.

Come up with a **unique** product or service, or **a unique twist/angle** to an existing product. Of course, the latter is much easier and quicker to do.

If you're in a highly competitive niche, take existing ideas and products and find ways to improve on them *considerably*. Find an area within your field/niche that needs attention but isn't getting any. Look for 'holes' in your niche. Figure out what the main problems and frustrations of customers that other marketers and business owners aren't addressing. You can find this by, doing surveys, visiting message boards and forums, etc.

Target a sub-niche (a smaller niche within a large niche) that isn't overflowing with competition, or one that isn't being addressed yet.

> Example: When I first got into online marketing, the 'spam' laws were just beginning to come about. Marketers were just starting to get away from sending unsolicited email because they didn't want to get in trouble. The online business was changing. New marketers were tip-toeing around the issue. They either got in trouble for sending unsolicited email, or were too afraid to even approach email marketing in fear of being labeled a 'spammer.'
>
> I noticed the area that needed attention: permission email marketing. Email marketing was the easiest and cheapest way to build a business. But people were too afraid to use it. They needed a step-by-step guide to using email marketing the 'right way' - using opt-in methods so they wouldn't get in trouble.

So, that's what I wrote about. **Email Marketing Strategies Revealed!** And, this is the book that put me on the map.

A really powerful way to come up with unique ideas is to study <u>other businesses</u> that are NOT related to your market. If you're in the online marketing field, look at the real estate business, the plumbing business or any other non-related business. If you look closely, with an open mind, you will find many creative and unique ideas that you can bring back to your own business and surprise your market! They will think you're a creative genius! ;-)

Don't hold back when you're trying to come up with new and creative ideas. Let your brain take off – freely and unhindered. Think back to when you were 8 years old. Get back in touch with that "nothing is impossible" energy that children possess. That can be your greatest ally in business.

Every now and then I'll come up with a completely original product idea, but *usually* it's just stuff I see happening around me. I look at what's already selling, what's already or is just starting to become popular.

I use my creativity to put new twists to existing "winning" ideas. That's the shortest route to success! By giving it a **twist**, it sort of becomes a unique product. Just learn to pay attention.

Keep one ear on the ground. Notice what's getting the most shelf space in bookstores. Visit discussion groups in your niche. Get on mailing lists, etc. In short, get out there and hang out among your customers and competitors (either online, offline, or both.) Do that and you'll never run out of ideas to write about.

However, I'd strongly recommend that you give your product idea a little "twist." Make it unique in some way so that it's not the same ole product that everyone else is selling. That little twist can make your product stand out and sell very well.

Here's an example from my past:

When I first started my „Secret Collection" of eBooks several years ago, no one was selling it the way I was. People were selling individual reports, on various niche subjects, but you rarely saw anyone put it together the way I had. And there was a reason no one was doing it.

It was difficult to group those products together and still maintain a "theme." Take for example subjects like online investigation, self defense, credit tips, beating speeding tickets and UFO"s. None of these products seem to have anything to do with each other. Or do they?

With a little creativity and some editing – yes they do. I put them into an eBook with a "secrets" **theme**. My main selling point and headline was; **"Discover Secrets You're Not Supposed To Know About!"** In the package, I revealed online investigative *secrets*, self defense *secrets*, credit *secrets*, UFO *secrets*... and so on. Suddenly, all these products - on different subjects that normally could not be grouped together - worked very well as a package. And even better people were interested and bought it.

I got the "package/membership site" idea from the Internet Marketing Warriors site. It wasn't an original idea but by paying attention, I duplicated something the top marketers were already doing. But, I gave it a twist that **was** original. At least for the online crowd.

You don't have to be an inventive genius to have a hot product. Just watch for what's selling.

Then, focus on solving problems, on providing solutions, on creating value for others, on making your product **better** than what's already out there, and you'll do great.

Power Tip: Here's another major reason for coming up with a unique product. Not only will the customers love your product but other businesses in your field/niche will become interested in working with you. Nothing can build your business faster than joint venturing (partnering) with other successful businesses. And nothing will get other businesses to want to partner with you more than a unique product that really solves the problem of your target market.

The Process

As soon as I get an idea for an eBook that gets me excited, I write it down. Keep a pen and pad, or tape recorder, with you at all times. Then, I transfer it into a 14" by 17" sketch pad. It's a drawing pad so there are no ruled lines.I designate at least one sheet to my new idea. And, then I just go crazy on it. The secret I've discovered is to forget about logic, linear thinking or organization. Just let go and pour out whatever is inside you at that moment.

In other words, my mind is usually going in 10 different directions when I scribble on the pad.

One minute I'm writing a brief table of contents on one section of the page. The next minute, I'm writing a killer headline that just came to me, for that product. Pretty soon this large 14" x 17" page is filled up with scribbles, notes, gems that I brainstormed. Everything that I can think of gets recorded, from the ads to the design to the actual content. I also let the idea simmer in the back of my head for a few days (and nights) and each time I get bits and pieces of insight, I make a note of them all.

(It's very important to let your mind relax and roam freely, in a limitless manner. That's when some awesome ideas can come to you. After you've given your brain a goal to focus on, sleep on the idea and let your brain really go to work on it, unhindered.)

Planning The Outline & Content

Since this report is about creating products **fast**, you'll notice me offering you some amazing shortcuts throughout this report that will help you get your eBook written super fast! To get my outline and content setup, I just go back to the sketch pad and play with it. I like to see everything laid out in front of me before I arrange them into any kind of order or sequence.

Of course, it doesn't have to be done on a large sketch pad, like I do. Find out what method works best for **you** and do that. You can just as easily create a document on your computer and start jotting down ideas for the book there. Basically, you want to make a note of all the sub-sections you will want to talk about. Then, when you're done listing these sections/chapters down, just arrange them in a sequence/order that makes sense. You've now got a table of contents, or at least the first draft of one.

Here's an easy way to get some ideas on creating an outline for your book: just look at the existing books on the subject! Whenever possible, try to use what's already out there, there's no point in reinventing the wheel. Go to the library and pick out a book on the subject you're writing about and see how they have it all laid out. DO NOT copy it. That's plagiarism and it'll get you in trouble. What you are doing is research, gathering ideas so that you can create your own masterpiece. If the book you're looking at has a good outline, you can model off of that. If the outlines (table of contents, etc.) are hard to follow on that book, you can improve on it when creating *your* eBook! It's a great way to a feel for what to do and also what **not** to do by looking at existing samples of work.

That should be the core mindset for you while you're creating your own products:

Make your product **better** than what is already out there!

I can't tell you how much time to spend per day on each chapter because I don't know what your lifestyle or schedule is like. Just spend some time working on the chapters, one at a time, and pretty soon you'll have the eBook completed.

Here's what I would suggest you do each time you sit down to work on your eBook: Look at the Table of Contents you've created and pick a subject/chapter that most interests you at that time. Work on that chapter!

You'll enjoy the process a lot more if you're writing about something that excites you at that moment. If you're excited about the subject you're writing about, your reader will feel that excitement while reading your eBook.

Avoiding Doubts, Fears, and Writers Block

When you're a beginner it's easy to doubt yourself. After all even seasoned writers still have to battle their fears and over come writers" block now and again. Here's a simple remedy: do whatever it takes to **shift your focus**. That's all there is to it.

Put the project aside for an hour or even a day if you have to. Go watch something funny on TV. Listen to your favorite music. Read a motivational book or article, play with the kids, or just go for a walk. It's really not as difficult as we often make it out to be. Just change the track your "train of thought" is currently riding on. Don't feel guilt for putting it off if you're just spinning your wheels, think of it more as regrouping so you come back fresh.

It also helps to envision the end result.

For example, if you'd like your book to earn you $50,000 per year, keep seeing/visualizing that result consistently, as if it has already happened! This process will burn the
"success" image into your brain and pretty soon, doubt will be a thing of the past.

Once you get excited about the end results you'll achieve, get back on the computer and start writing!

Proper Layout and Design

Don't make it hard on yourself, especially if this is your first eBook. Just go out there and look for the best sellers related to your subject. Study the best ones and find out **why** they are the best. What is it about them that are appealing to **you**? Then, use those formats as *models*.

Here's an easy way to make your eBook easy to read: **suck the reader in**! Most how-to books are dry and boring, with just a list of facts and figures. Make yours entertaining too, if possible. Keep this in mind:

> "It's not the *story* that makes it a hit. It's how the story is *told*!"

See, anyone can write a book that delivers facts and figures. But few people can write a book that others will want to read. This is why it's so important to be passionate and excited about the subject you're writing about. It's also why you want to write in a conversational tone instead of the rigid formal tone. You don't want to sound like a text books.

Inject your personality into the eBook. If you have a great sense of humor, give your readers a taste of that. Be yourself; if you try to be somebody you're not, your eBook will sound unnatural.

Pricing

How do you decide what the best selling price is for your eBook? Again, look at what's already out there. **Research is your biggest ally in this business**. See what other sellers are charging for their products and look at the sales page to find out what they're offering in exchange for that price. And whenever possible, I take a look at the actual products others are selling, to see how well they're done and if they are worth the asking price.

Then, there are several ways you can use that information. Here's an example...

If most people are charging $47 for the standard info on the subject, you should aim on offering:

1) a better product/package, and

2) a better deal/offer.

You can either offer the same or similar information for say $39.97... or you can keep the price at $47 but add some valuable bonuses to the package to increase the perceived value of the overall package or provide additional useful info in your main product that other people are not offering. Make yours better!

Promoting Your Book To The World

If you have an existing mailing list, tell them about your new eBook first! Offer them the best deal possible – a special offer that no one else will be getting. Treat your own list the best and tell them that you are. Offer your customers an affiliate program so they can promote the product to others while they earn a commission.

If you don't have your own list start sending out „joint venture" offers to other businesses in your field. Offer them a nice-sized commission (at least 50%) and explain to them how they (*as well as their customers*) will benefit from the deal. Send out at least one JV letter, **per day**! Joint ventures with other marketers and business owners can pull in amazing profits! They're the best promoting tool available for writers and marketers -- especially online!

You can also use highly-targeted ezine ads to get customers. Here's a twist to this technique: **instead of targeting customers, target affiliates who will help you sell the product!** This strategy can grow your business very quickly!

If you don't have an existing customer list here's another strategy that can work well. Write short, focused articles and submit them to targeted ezines. Articles can be a great way to get viral advertising working for you.

There are hundreds of other strategies you can use. However, the ones listed above are some of the best and most effective. Always go for „quality" traffic verses „quantity."

What To Do When You Get Stuck

If you get stuck or lost at any point during the product creation / marketing process, don't panic. There's an easy solution! Just watch what the experts in your field are doing and how they're doing it. Then do the same thing. For example, if you can't think of a great title for your eBook, look to the experts. Or, go to amazon.com and do a search for books on that subject. Read the titles/headlines and you'll get some great ideas from there.

If you're having a hard time creating a killer sales letter for your product, look at the top sellers and see how they're doing it. Model yours after the best sellers!

Don't *steal* their work, but you'll be surprised at how inspired you will be to go write your own after reading some that work. And of course, **make yours better**! □

Another good point to keep in mind is... your book doesn't have to be hundreds of pages long. I tend to create short powerful reports because they are quick and easy to produce.

That's a great way to go, especially if you're a new marketer and want to get your feet wet. Best of all, short reports allow you to spread your risk, all of your projects will not become home runs, that's the reality of any business. If you invest a lot of time and energy into creating a monster eBook that turns out to be a dud, you'll become discouraged. On the other hand, if you had only spent *a few weeks* on creating a much shorter eBook which also turned out to be a dud, you could quickly pull that one out and replace it with another short one. Your risks are dramatically reduced and your chances of putting out a winner are increased!

It's better to create 10 little eBooks per year and have 2 of them flop (which means 8 of them are bringing in the cash!) than to only create one or two **big** eBooks in that same year and risk having them both flop. There is also a much better chance that 1 of your products will be a hot seller if you have 10 of them out there, instead of just one or two.

That has been my strategy for the past 7+ years. And it has worked very well for me. It can work well for you too.

Make It Better!

Most importantly, keep testing and tracking everything you do! After you have the basics down, start testing everything to make it **better**. Test your headlines to see which one pulls better. Test your offer, packaging, benefits, pricing... test everything! Don't let anyone tell you what they "think" will work. Let your customers decide that for you. Don't ever stop improving on what you have. Each little improvement you make can mean substantial *additional* profits for you. It's the easiest way I know of to give your self a raise without doing too much extra work.

Finally, make your package <u>unique</u>, either through the offer, the packaging, or the product itself. Make yours stand out from the rest of the pack. If you don't do that, you'll be lost among the other mediocre offers, and your customers will probably never find you.

(If you can't think of a way to make your product/offer unique, just look at how other *industries* are doing it. You'll get some great ideas just by watching other businesses that are completely unrelated to your field.)

Do the above and you'll *continue* to get great results.

Speaking of being unique, if you're thinking of writing an eBook on marketing, **DON'T!** Pick any other subject. You'll have a much easier time selling a product outside of the „marketing" arena. You'll also often have **much less competition** in the non-marketing niches, and a much greater profit potential.

I guarantee your mind will start racing with all kinds of ideas just by looking at the contents inside the above site. □□

I wish you much success in all your future endeavors.

Recommended Payment Processors

PayPal – the most used and recognized merchant in the Internet marketplace.

Recommended Web Hosting

HostGator - Hostgator allows unlimited WordPress installation and it is one of the cheapest and reliable web hosting out there. See HostGator coupon codes here.

Recommended Marketing Resources

WordPressRiver.com - is a free tutorial site for WordPress users packed with video tutorials as well as fully illustrated guides.

PLR Mines – Gain lifetime access to a collection of TOP quality Resell Rights products, Private Label products, templates, auto responders, Advanced Reseller Strategies, and much more, as a Gold member!

Other Marketing Resources

PremadeThemes - ready made niche WordPress themes for your niche marketing needs.

About The Author:

*Name: **Mr. Joseph O Iredia**,*
Contents writer, Blogger, Affiliate Marketer
and Web designer.

Website Address: *www.letmoneypay.com*
Email: *info@letmoneypay.com*